Official Rules and Play

CANASTA

(BASKET RUMMY)

by JOSEFINA ARTAYETA DE VIEL, *Club Argentino de Bridge, Buenos Aires*

Approved by an Argentine Commission headed by ALEJANDRO CASTRO

Foreword by FLORENCE OSBORN

Author of *How's Your Bridge Game?*

Introduction by RALPH MICHAELS

PELLEGRINI & CUDAHY, *New York*

Contents

FOREWORD by Florence Osborn.................. 5

WHY CANASTA 7

INTRODUCTION by Ralph Michaels.............. 9

RULES OF PLAY 13

    I. THE PLAYERS 13

    II. THE CARDS 13

    III. THE DEAL 13

    IV. THE PLAY 15

        The Draw 15

        The Meld 16

        The Discard 18

    V. BONUSES 20

    VI. DEFINITIONS 21

        Canastas 21

        Red Treys 21

        Black Treys 21

        Up-Pile 22

        Prize Pile......................... 22

        Melding Out 23

        Concealed Hand 23

        Permission to Go Out............... 24

    VII. PENALTIES 25

    VIII. ALTERNATIVES 26

TIPS ON PLAY................................ 27

Foreword

CANASTA IS THE GAME OF THE HOUR. NEWLY IMPORTED from South America, where it is played with great skill and enthusiasm, Canasta is rapidly becoming a favorite card game of players here and abroad.

Canasta, or basket in Spanish, is an exciting and highly developed· form · of the universal favorite, Rummy, which is one of our oldest card games and can be traced back 400 years to a game called Conquian, also of Spanish origin. Thus the new game, belonging as it does to the old, is at once pleasingly familiar and easy to understand.

Canasta was played first in Uruguay, as far as we know, and was quickly adopted by the card-loving Argentines who added refinements and brought it with them as summer visitors to this country. It is finding friends in Paris, New York, Newport, Washington and Hollywood, and bids fair to overtake all Gin Rummy players.

Rummy itself is a wonderful two-handed game which fills with pleasure an evening at home, and in the form of Canasta can easily be expanded to include three, four or six players with added enjoyment.

Cards are one means of bridging differences in age

and habits, drawing children and parents, old and new friends together in fair and friendly competition.

I play Rummy with my little girl and boy almost every evening after dinner. It gives us something to do together which is fun and at which they have a chance at beating me (figuratively speaking, of course). I am planning to teach them Canasta as soon as I am sure I know the rules myself.

Mrs. Josefina Artayeta de Viel, of Buenos Aires, who has mothered Canasta from an infant when it was first taken up by her Argentine friends, and Mr. Ralph Michaels, of Chicago, who is her enthusiastic sponsor, have worked earnestly to give you here a clear, simple and correct explanation of the game as it is played in the land where it was born, South America.

Either for friends or family, or both, Canasta you will find is a great game.

Florence Osborn

(Florence Osborn is bridge editor of the New York *Herald Tribune* and author of the book, *How's Your Bridge Game?*)

Why Canasta

SOME TIME AGO WE RECEIVED A CALL FROM A STRANGER asking if we would be interested in publishing a book on a new card game. Both the enthusiasm of the caller and the fascination of a new field aroused our curiosity.

We soon learned that this new game, CANASTA, was first played in Montevideo, Uruguay. It was known as CANASTA URUGUAYA, or in English "Uruguayan Basket."

It did not take long for this game to cross the Plata River and become popular in Argentina. While traveling with his wife in Argentina, a young Chicago businessman, Ralph Michaels, first saw CANASTA played in the Buenos Aires home of Lewis and Rosalind Fremont, two internationally known Bridge players. The Michaels were soon playing top notch CANASTA and teaching it to their Chicago friends.

On one of their return trips from South America, they taught some players who in turn introduced the game in Newport and New York. Once the game was played in New York it began to grow like a snowball. Because CANASTA was being popularized by word of mouth and handed down from one player to another, each transition led to slight modifications and improvisations. It was not long before the methods of

7

play of CANASTA were as many and varied as Gin Rummy when that game was first introduced to the card-playing public. Even the players of the various South American groups found that differences of play existed.

It was logical that local rules had to be determined before the game could be played properly nationally and internationally. In order to standardize the play, Josefina Artayeta de Viel, eminent card authority and editor of one of the Argentine magazines, was requested to compile a standard set of rules and play for CANASTA. These rules were then edited and adopted by the following committee as the official rules covering the play of CANASTA:

ALEJANDRO CASTRO —

International card authority and President of the Argentine Bridge Players Association

DR. JORGE ARTAYETA —

President of the Circulo de Armas, one of Buenos Aires' most exclusive clubs

DR. PEDRO PALACIOS —

President of Argentine Bridge Club

SRA. DORA BRUSAFERRO DE DODERO —

Eminent Argentine card authority

It is these original Argentine rules that we herewith present.

Introduction

FOR THOSE WHO THINK THEY HAVE TRIED WILD RUMMY
games, let us start by saying "wild" is only a mild adjective when used in connection with CANASTA. CANASTA
embodies the principles of building card combinations
as in GIN, the melding of PINOCLE, the partnership understanding of BRIDGE, and deception of POKER, plus the
offense, defense, and cunning of competitive sports. If
you love your neighbor, don't play CANASTA with him.

If you have played any sort of Rummy, CANASTA will
not be too difficult for you to learn. One thing is urged,
however, beyond all else — do not attempt to play until
you have digested *all* the rules of this booklet. Once you
start to play, you will see the wisdom of this advice.
It's no use learning to take off in an airplane if you
don't also learn to land the contraption; CANASTA is
not too different; know all the rules first.

Although CANASTA can be played with two, three,
four, or six players, it is particularly exciting as a
four-handed game of two opposing partnerships and
also a most deceptive two-handed game.

In CANASTA the individual cards and various combinations of cards have point values. The objective of
the game is to amass 5,000 or more of these points be-

9

fore your opponents. The quickest and most profitable
method of accumulating these points is by melding and
building towards Canastas. A Canasta is a set of seven
cards of the same rank, regardless of suit (i.e., seven
fours, seven fives, seven kings, etc.). This is not so im-
possible as it sounds when you realize that CANASTA is
played with two standard decks of cards shuffled together with four jokers, *and* every deuce is a wild card.

In building towards the objective of 5,000 points,
it will soon be seen that the premiums are greatest for
Canastas, hence the emphasis in the play is not so much
to meld out which is so important in GIN, but rather
to continue the play to acquire more Canastas. At the
same time, however, it is of the utmost importance
to prevent the opponent from doing likewise. Thus
we have both an offense and a defense.

Like most Rummy games, there is both a stock pile
(the undealt cards placed in the center of the table
face down) and a discard pile (also placed in the center
of the table but face up — in CANASTA called "up-pile").
In CANASTA the value of the cards is insignificant compared with the value of Canastas. Since it takes seven
cards to complete a Canasta, the tactics of the game
center around control of the up-pile. The player or
team in control of the up-pile has the best chance for
the greater number of Canastas.

It has been known to happen that 5,000 points has
been reached in the play of only one deal or hand.
The more usual, however, is to reach this goal through
the play of a succession of hands. Like other types of
Rummy, a hand is ended when one of the players

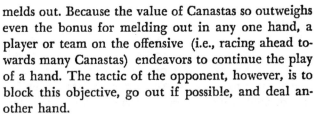

melds out. Because the value of Canastas so outweighs even the bonus for melding out in any one hand, a player or team on the offensive (i.e., racing ahead towards many Canastas) endeavors to continue the play of a hand. The tactic of the opponent, however, is to block this objective, go out if possible, and deal another hand.

The merciless feature of CANASTA is the rapidity with which the offensive team can become the defensive team. The excitement of this can best be compared to the elation of one side and dejection of the other when in football a forward pass is intercepted and returned for a touchdown. You, as a player, will soon realize this part of the game the first time you are trapped. In Poker "sandbagging" is often outlawed. Not so in CANASTA! Just the opposite! You must learn to hold up melds, make false discards, end play your opponent, and employ all the deceptive tactics at your command. It is probably this feature of deception that makes CANASTA so appealing to a Bridge or Poker player.

With 108 cards to account for, the probabilities of hands are up in the billions. Likewise the choice of plays, even for experts, is not always clear cut. When to attack, when to defend, when to meld, when to hold up are all important single theoretical features of CANASTA which could be classified as "timing," which only experience can teach. A new situation will pop up every time you play the game. To be an expert, therefore, you cannot play too often.

I see that in writing this introduction I have con-

centrated as much on "how to play" as "why play."
Perhaps you have gathered a hint of "why play." Of
course, one's first love in cards should be for a friendly
game. If, however, you can leave out the friendship
angle, turn to CANASTA. And when you start your first
hand, don't say you weren't warned. Psychiatrists love
this game — it produces so many patients!

Ralph Michaels

RULES AND PLAY OF
CANASTA

CANASTA, or basket, is a type of rummy. The object of the game is to reach or exceed 5,000 points before one's opponents. The winnings and losings are computed by the differences in the total scores of the opposing players or teams.

I. PLAYERS

The game may be played by two, three, four, or six players. If played by two or three, each plays for his individual account; if played by four, there are two sets of partners, each person facing his partner at the table; if played by six, there are two sets of partners with three players each, seated alternately at the table.

II. CARDS

Two decks of standard playing cards of fifty-two cards each and four jokers are used. The four jokers and eight deuces are wild cards. Since the various suits are not used in CANASTA, the cards held in the hand should be assorted according to numerical values.

III. THE DEAL

A. Players cut for deal and choice of seats. High card has choice of seats, next highest (in case of three players) has second choice. When there are four players, the drawers of the two highest cards are partners; in six-

13

handed, the three highest are partners. The right-hand* opponent of the drawer of the highest card shuffles the two decks together and, after his righthand opponent has cut, deals clockwise. The deal passes to the left after each hand is finished until the game ends. The players may then either 1) cut again, or 2) change partners, the dealer and his lefthand opponent remaining in their places. In the latter case, at the end of the second game, the dealer remains in his place and takes as his partner the one of the other three with whom he has not played; and at the end of the third game, the players must cut again. For the purposes of the cut, the joker has no value and another card must be drawn; the deuce is the lowest card, then the trey, etc.; the suits (for the cut only) rank upwards: Clubs, Diamonds, Hearts, and Spades.

B. Each player is dealt eleven cards, one at a time. Fifteen cards are dealt to each player in two-handed; and thirteen in three-handed. The remainder of the cards are placed face down in the center of the table and become the stock pile. Red treys are exposed, placed on the table before a player or his partner, and the top card of the stock pile is drawn to replace such exposed red treys. Should another red trey be drawn, it is like-

---

Publisher's Note: The rules of CANASTA as played in Argentina employ a counter-clockwise method of dealing and playing to the right. This, we felt, was so awkward that we took the liberty of rewording all such directions to the more common clockwise system.

wise exposed immediately and replaced before the turn
to replace passes to the lefthand player.

C. The dealer turns the top card of the stock pile
face up to start the up-pile. If the up-card proves to be
a red trey or a wild card, the dealer must cover it with
the next card from the stock pile until a natural card
is the up-card. The player to the left of the dealer has
the option of taking the up-pile (if he is able to do so)
or drawing the top card of the stock pile. The privilege
of taking the up-card on the deal does not pass to the
other players.

IV. THE PLAY

The play commences with the player to the left of the
dealer and consists of three parts:

1. The Draw
2. The Meld (optional)
3. The Discard

A. *The Draw*

1. On the first play, the player to the left of the dealer
may take the up-pile only if he has two cards matching
the up-card in rank and the sufficient amount of meld.
The up-card, but no other card in the up-pile, may
count towards this amount of meld. The player must
expose the cards to be melded from his hand before
taking up the up-pile. The up-card MUST be melded
on the table; the remainder of the up-pile may be
kept in the hand. (See B below for rules and count on
melding.)

2. Once a player or his partner has melded, he may take the up-pile with one matching natural card and a wild card; or he may take the pile when the up-card can be added to an exposed meld, except in the case of a prize pile described below. The up-card can never be taken to play with only two or more wild cards.

3. A player with only one card in his hand cannot take an up-pile consisting of only one card.

4. The up-pile becomes a prize pile when it contains a red trey or a wild card. It can be taken *only* with two matching cards concealed in the hand. It cannot be taken with one matching card and a wild card, nor may it be taken when the up-card is playable on the exposed meld. Of course, should the player have two or more concealed matching cards of an exposed meld, he may take the matching up-card of a prize pile.

5. If a player does not take the up-pile, he draws the top card of the stock pile. Taking the up-pile, even though he is able to do so, is optional.

B. *The Meld*

MINIMUM COUNT REQUIRED FOR FIRST MELD

When score is:	Required Meld
Minus	15 points
from 0 to 1495	50 points
from 1500 to 2995	90 points
from 3000 to 4995	120 points

VALUE OF CARDS

Jokers	50 points
Deuces	20 points
Aces	20 points
8 spot thru King	10 points
Black trey thru 7 spot	5 points

1. A meld is a set of three or more cards of the same rank, regardless of suit. (Sequences are never used.) At least two natural cards are needed for an initial meld. Once a player or his partner has melded the initial amount, either partner may add cards to their exposed melds during subsequent plays until one player has melded out or the stock pile is exhausted. Adding cards to an opponent's meld is never permitted. The exposed melds, together with the red treys of a partnership, are accumulated together in front of one of the partners.

2. The Canasta, or basket, is composed of seven cards of the same rank. At least four of the cards in a Canasta must be natural. For the purpose of a Canasta, a wild card takes the rank of the cards with which it is melded, but retains its own value for the card count. Once melded it cannot be changed. No more than three wild cards are permitted in a meld. Once the Canasta is completed, its cards are folded together. In the case of a natural Canasta, a red card is placed at the top; in the case of a mixed Canasta (one which contains wild cards) a natural black card is placed on top, as there is a difference in the bonus given at the end of the play. When the Canasta has been closed, natural cards may

be added during subsequent plays; these do not change the bonus for the Canasta but have value only in the card count. Wild cards may also be added to a closed Canasta but not if the Canasta already contains three. If a wild card is added to a closed natural Canasta (which may happen when a player wishes to meld out), the Canasta becomes a mixed Canasta.

3. Black treys may be melded only to go out; as discards they are stop cards, and the up-pile may never be taken when a black trey is the up-card. If melded, they count as indicated above. Red treys are merely bonus cards (value explained later) and have no point value in the card count.

4. A player melds out when he disposes of all his cards either by melding them or by melding all except one, which he may discard. His side must have at least one Canasta, or he must complete one in melding out.

C. *The Discard*.

1. When a player has completed his play, he must discard one card, except when he melds out and a discard is optional. Wild cards and black treys are stop cards, and the up-pile can not be taken when one of these is the up-card. When a player is left with only one card, he must announce it by knocking on the table. It is permissible to ask a partner or opponent how many cards he is holding.

2. The player who draws the last card of the stock pile must discard unless he melds out. Should this discard be playable on the exposed melds of the lefthand

opponent, this opponent is obliged to take the up-card, meld it on his exposed meld, and take the balance of the up-pile. This obligation to take the up-pile is nullified only when it conflicts with the rule which states that a player who has no more than one card in his hand may not take an up-pile of one card. This continuance of play after exhausting the stock pile is called "forcing." A player who is "forced" must naturally take the up-card and then discard. This discard in turn may be a "force" card, i.e., a card playable on the lefthand opponent's exposed melds. Thus play continues until one of the players discards a card which is not playable by his lefthand opponent. During a "force," should the up-card be playable with cards concealed in a hand, the player may take it if he wishes; if not, the hand is ended.

3. In case the last card of the stock pile is a red trey (which obviously cannot be replaced), the hand is automatically ended and neither side receives the 100 point bonus.

4. When the first player has completed his turn to draw, meld and discard, the play moves on in order to the left.

V. BONUSES

A. The bonuses earned by a player or partnership are credited to their score in accordance with the following table:

Canasta (Natural)	500 points each
Canasta (Mixed)	300 points each
Red Treys	100 points each
Red Treys — 4 on one side	200 points each
Hand Bonus	100 points each
Concealed Hand Bonus	100 points each

B. At the conclusion of each hand the bonus points (Canastas, red treys, and hand bonus) arè first counted and credited to the respective sides. The value of the cards left in the players' hands plus any penalties which may have been accrued during the hand are then deducted from the value of the cards contained in the exposed melds. (Note that meldable cards concealed in the hands are included in the deduction.) The net value of the cards of one side plus its bonus points are added together and the game continued until the total scores of the hands reach or exceed 5,000 points. Each hand is played to the end even though 5,000 points may have been reached during the hand. In case more than one player exceeds 5,000 points at the end of a hand, the one with the greater number of points is declared the winner.

VI. DEFINITIONS

A. *Canastas*

A Canasta is a set of seven cards of the same rank regardless of suit, melded by a player, or a player and his partners. It may be either natural or mixed. Completed Canastas are differentiated by topping a natural Canasta with a red card and a mixed Canasta with a natural black card.

1. A "natural Canasta" consists of seven cards of the same rank without any wild cards.

2. A "mixed Canasta" consists of a set of seven cards made up of natural cards of the same rank and one or more wild cards. A mixed Canasta must have at least four natural cards and no more than three wild cards.

B. *Red Treys*

The red treys are bonus cards and must be exposed immediately and replaced by a card from the stock pile. The red trey has no value in the card count, but carries a bonus of 100 points each, or 800 for all four on one side. If a hand ends before a side has melded, the red treys it owns are counted AGAINST this side in the same amounts. Red treys taken in prize piles are exposed but not replaced.

C. *Black Treys*

The discard of a black trey stops the lefthand opponent from taking the up-pile on that play; no up-pile can be taken when a black trey is the up-card. Black treys can be melded only to go out when three or four of them are concealed in a hand. They cannot be melded with a wild card. They have a value of 5 points in the card count.

D. *Up-Pile*

The up-pile is the collection of cards discarded by the players. It may be taken when the up-card can be melded. If neither a player nor his partner has melded, it can be taken with two matching natural cards when the player has the required amount. Only the up-card can be counted towards the amount required to meld. If a player or his partner has melded, the up-pile can be taken with one matching card and a wild card, a pair, or if the up-card is playable on an exposed meld, including Canastas. The up-card must always be played, and the sufficient amount from the player's hand placed on the table, before the remainder of the up-pile is taken into the hand.

The up-pile must be kept one card on top of the other so that not more than the top card is exposed. Players are not permitted to see more than the top exposed card.

E. *Prize Pile*

The up-pile becomes a prize pile when it contains a wild card or a red trey. This pile can be taken only with a concealed natural pair. At the beginning of the game, should the up-card be a wild card or a red trey, it is immediately covered with the top card of the stock pile, and the game continues under the rules of the prize pile until the pile has been taken. During the game any player may discard a wild card thereby making the up-pile a prize pile. Subsequently, any player may, as often as wished, discard another wild card into the same prize pile. A wild card so played becomes a stop card for the lefthand opponent who is obliged to draw from the stock pile.

A prize pile cannot be taken even though a subsequent up-card is playable on an exposed meld, unless the player also has a matching pair in his hand (i.e., you have an exposed meld of jacks; a jack is discarded and becomes the up-card of a prize pile; you may not take this prize pile unless you have a natural pair of jacks concealed in your hand).

F. *Melding Out*

The person to meld out in each hand receives a bonus of 100 points. If the stock pile has been exhausted and the last discard cannot be played by the lefthand opponent during "forcing," and neither team has gone out, the hand is automatically ended. In such cases the score is counted, but neither team receives the 100 point hand bonus. There is no bonus for winning the game.

G. *Concealed Hand*

A concealed hand is one in which a player goes out without previously melding on the table. This may be done in one of two ways:

1. By playing on his partner's exposed melds. In this case the side must either have previously made a Canasta or the player completes a Canasta during his melding out.

2. By melding out with a Canasta concealed in the hand. In this case the required amount for melding is waived.

(The bonus for a concealed hand is 100 points in addi-
tion to the 100 point hand bonus.)

H. *Permission to Go Out*

1. When a player desires to end a hand and meld out, it is customary to ask his partner: "Shall I go out?" The question is asked after the player has drawn from the stock pile but before he has made a play from his hand. The question may be repeated by either partner during subsequent plays.

2. The partner of the asker must reply simply by either "yes" or "no" and such decision is final and binding for this play. The asking of permission to go out must take place *after* the draw from the stock pile but *before* a play from the hand. If a player should ask permission *during* the play of cards from his hand, he may not go out regardless of partner's answer and his side is penalized 200 points (Penalty D).

3. The asking of permission is not obligatory, for when a player considers it expedient to go out, or his hand is such he cannot safely continue play, he may go out without asking. A player may never ask to go out after having drawn the up-pile (Penalty D).

4. In six-handed, permission is asked of the left-hand partner. His answer is binding for this play of the team.

VII. PENALTIES

A. Misdeal — the penalty for a misdeal is 100 points. If 12 cards have been dealt to each of the players and they have seen their cards, there is no penalty, but one round is played in which case each discards but does not draw; the play then proceeds normally. In all other misdeals the cards must be redealt by the same dealer.

B. Melding with insufficient count has a penalty of 100 points, and the player is obliged to discard one of the cards contained in his meld. If the player has drawn from the up-pile, the card so drawn must be returned, a draw made from the stock pile, then a discard of one of his melded cards, and the balance of the meld is returned to his concealed hand.

C. If an up-pile containing more than two cards is improperly taken, the penalty is 100 points.

D. Any observation indicating a player's own holding or directing the partner's play carries a penalty of 200 points.

E. If the question "Shall I go out?" is asked and the player is unable to do so, the penalty is 200 points. In a two- or three-handed game a player who erroneously indicates he is out, or erroneously proclaims himself out, is penalized 200 points.

F. For failure to expose a red trey the penalty is 500 points.

G. A play out of turn is penalized 100 points.

H. The erroneous inclusion of more than three wild cards in a Canasta nullifies the 300 point bonus.

VIII. ADDENDA

1. It is never permissible for a player to discard all his cards, except with the intention of melding out. The player must have at least one card in his hand at all times during play. Remember too that no player may meld out without a Canasta (see Section F, page 23).

2. In making an initial meld, it is permissible to meld as many combinations as desired. Good strategy, however, dictates that the player hold these to a minimum — for example, A-A-joker = 90 points; 5-5-5-5-2 + 10-10-10-2 equals the same number of points, as does also Q-Q-Q + K-K-K + J-J-J.

TIPS ON PLAY

A. The three most important points for a player to remember are the meld, the taking of the up-pile, and the defense of the discard pile.

1. It is fundamental in all rummy games to arrive at a combination of cards that results in a good meld. In Canasta it is highly important to meld since:

    a. The values of the cards on the board count towards the score instead of against, as they do in the hand.

    b. If a side has red treys, they become an asset only after a meld.

    c. Even though one's partner is unable to reach the count for the required meld, he may have complementary cards that will ensure or assist the making of a Canasta.

    d. A side that has melded has more chance to take the up-pile.

2. The taking of the up-pile gives more playing cards while keeping them from the opponent. With these extra playing cards comes greater chance to take future up-piles, open up new melds and make more Canastas. This does not mean that worthless up-piles should be taken at the sacrifice of wild cards, especially if there is a scarcity of the latter.

3. It follows that the defense of the up-pile, by playing stop cards or cards unlikely to be taken, is of ex-

treme importance. Remember the cards in the up-pile and bear in mind that even though they may seem worthless they may have great value for the opponent

4. It may sometimes be advisable, when the opponents show a decided advantage in a hand, to discard a playable card, even though it would complete a Canasta for the opponents, rather than break up a hand and ruin the possibilities of going out.

B. If wild cards must be used in melding, it is better to play two melds instead of one since only three wild cards are permitted in a Canasta.

C. It is wise to complete a Canasta rather quickly. The timing for this depends on how close the opponents are to making a Canasta. Remember, neither side can go out on a hand without first completing a Canasta. After completing your first Canasta, it may prove more strategic to conceal cards in the hand, such as keeping pairs of exposed melds in case a wild card is discarded and the up-pile becomes a prize pile.

D. The perfect initial play is one in which you can make a meld of the initial count and discard a black trey to stop the up-pile to your lefthand opponent, giving your partner the first chance at the up-pile.

E. Remember, the most important playing factor in CANASTA is *timing*. This feature of the game cannot be taught — it must be acquired through frequent practice. In every play, remember your TIMING.

F. During the course of play a player should shift the type of hand he holds, depending on whether the up-pile is a prize pile or not. If there is a prize pile, one should naturally keep pairs concealed in the hand. If it is not a prize pile and one has a wild card, it is most advantageous to keep a variety of unrelated cards in the hand in order to be in a better position to take advantage of almost any discard by one's right hand opponent.

G. When a player's concealed cards are playable on the opponents' melds and he is "squeezed" or he sees that his partner is in this situation, he should play a wild card to stop the up-pile and make it a prize pile.

H. When nearing the end of the stock pile, try to save a stop card to play if it is desirable to prevent the opponents from continuing the game. If it is advantageous to force them to continue the play, save cards that are playable on the opponents' melds.

I. In order to make more than one Canasta, it is important not to get down to too few cards as it is better to make extra Canastas than merely get the 100 point bonus for going out. When partner has few cards and you have many, it is prudent to pass up an opportunity to take the up-pile in order to give your partner this chance to accumulate more cards.

J. The play of certain cards can often be interpreted as a signal from one partner to another. Early in the game, prior to making one's initial meld, the play by one of the partners of a black trey usually indicates either that the player is in trouble and is begging his partner to make the initial meld or that he is very close to the count and partner should exercise caution. A most important signal is the play of a wild card as the fifth or sixth card on an exposed meld; this is a plea to partner to help complete this Canasta.

K. If your partner makes the initial meld, it is often prudent to hold up plays from your hand a round or so in order to trap the opponents into discarding a card which might match those in your hand, thereby giving you a desirable pile.

L. Do not play your black treys too quickly. Save them for use as stop cards at a time when the up-pile is more desirable.

M. Towards the end of the game if it looks as if the stock pile will be exhausted and one of the players will commence "forcing," it is most advantageous to get the black treys. This is both offensive and defensive. Thus, if you are player, or partner of a player, who is going to "force," you must get hold of the black treys so that your opponents will not have the opportunity to end the hand. Conversely, if you are the opponent on the defensive against a player or team which is endeavoring to get in a "forcing" position, an effort should be made to obtain the black treys in order to end the hand.

N. Keep close watch on the score. Your position with regard to reaching the game of 5000 points often influences your desire to go out or with respect to your partner's asking to go out. This is also true as a defensive measure in preventing the opponents from reaching game.

O. Don't be too hasty to add playable cards on closed Canastas. These cards often prove valuable for discarding purposes.

P. Take advantage of the rules permitting one to ask partner's permission to go out and asking other players how many cards they hold. These two questions during the play of a hand often have great strategic value.

See next page for sample score sheet

————————————————————————————————————

Fill in your name and address, and mail this coupon to the publisher to assure your receiving new rulings on CANASTA. Mr. Ralph Michaels will answer questions of play addressed to him care of the publisher; please enclose a self-addressed stamped envelope.

Pellegrini & Cudahy
333 Sixth Avenue
New York 14, New York

NAME . . . .

ADDRESS . . . .

CITY . . . . STATE . . . .

Canasta

D	We	They	D	We	They	D	We	They

COLUMN D for dealers initials

PELLEGRINI & CUDAHY, INC.
333 Sixth Avenue, New York 14

CPSIA information can be obtained
at www.ICGtesting.com
Printed in the USA
BVHW051224280223
659295BV00020BB/75